Embracing ADHD

Navigating Life With A Unique Mind

Crystal A. Bowen

Disclaimer

The outline's contents are never to supersede the book but rather to assist Readers in figuring out an intelligent read.

This outline has been generally prepared to nail down the critical core themes and truths and to aid in gaining an understanding; you may interpret the book.

Have A Good Read!!!

Table Of Contents

Introduction: My ADHD Journey – A Personal And Universal Story

My Discovery And Diagnosis

My adventure with ADHD started in a way not unique to many adults. It was a sequence of missed signs, misunderstandings, and a continual sensation of being out of pace with the world around me.

For years, I wandered through life with an unseen companion whose name I didn't know, one who made routine chores extraordinarily hard and left me feeling chronically burdened.

The moment of discovery occurred unexpectedly in my thirties, following a normal appointment to a psychotherapist for what I believed was anxiety.

After a series of inquiries and reflections on my childhood and adult life, the phrase 'ADHD' was first introduced. It was like a jigsaw piece snapping into place, a moment of clarity amid a lifetime of bewilderment.

The diagnosis was a surprise, and yet, it came with a freight of emotions - relief, confusion, and a terrifying feeling of uncertainty about what this meant for my future.

The Challenge Of Understanding ADHD

Understanding ADHD was like learning a new language, one that explained my history and enlightened my present. The immediate comfort of diagnosis quickly gave way to grasping what ADHD meant.

The preconceptions of hyperactive children were far distant from my experience as an adult battling with inattention, time management, and a persistent feeling of underachievement.

Embarking on this road of enlightenment meant deconstructing years of entrenched misunderstandings. I had to study the range of ADHD manifestations, how it varied in adults, especially in women, and how its symptoms were sometimes misinterpreted for character faults or a lack of effort.

This information was not only scholarly; it was extremely personal. It necessitated reliving many difficult incidents of my life under a fresh light, knowing that what I had considered as personal failings were, in reality, signs of a neurological illness.

The Purpose Of This Book

This book is formed out of a desire to share my path - not because it is exceptional, but exactly because it is not. My tale is one of millions, each as different as the symptoms of ADHD itself.

This book seeks to be a companion on your path, whether you are recently diagnosed, believe you may have ADHD, or are someone trying to understand a loved one who does.

The objective of this work is threefold. Firstly, it tries to bring clarity where there is uncertainty, to provide a window into the ADHD mind for people who live with it and those who live beside it. Secondly, this book is a toolbox, gathering tactics, insights, and coping mechanisms that have helped me and many others manage life with ADHD.

Finally, this book is an invitation to talk, to form a community where experiences are exchanged and understanding is expanded.

As we continue on this journey together, remember that knowing ADHD is not only about detecting symptoms; it's about appreciating the depth and complexity of the ADHD experience.

It's about finding strength in our uniqueness and learning to succeed, not despite ADHD but because of the distinct perspective it provides to our lives.

Chapter One: Understanding ADHD – Beyond The Stereotypes

Debunking Common Myths

Attention Deficit Hyperactivity Disorder (ADHD) is a disorder clouded in misconceptions and myths, sometimes reinforced by media depictions and cultural misunderstandings.

One of the most common beliefs is that ADHD is primarily a childhood condition marked by hyperactivity and behavioral issues. However, ADHD is significantly more complicated and nuanced, impacting people over their lives in unique ways. Another prevalent myth is that ADHD is a consequence of bad parenting or lack of discipline.

This misconception undermines the neurological foundation of ADHD and disregards the genetic and biological elements involved. It also imposes an extra load of shame and blame on families already trying to assist a loved one with ADHD.

Perhaps one of the most destructive fallacies is the assumption that ADHD is not a serious medical illness but rather an excuse for laziness or inattentiveness.

This myth invalidates the actual issues experienced by persons with ADHD and overlooks decades of scientific study and clinical data confirming the authenticity of the illness.

The Science Of ADHD

To properly comprehend ADHD, one must go into the science underlying it. ADHD is a neurodevelopmental condition characterized by patterns of inattention, hyperactivity, and impulsivity.

From a neurological aspect, ADHD is linked with variations in brain structure and function, notably in regions related to attention, executive function, and impulse control.

Research suggests that ADHD has a strong hereditary component, with the probability of a kid developing ADHD greatly raised if a parent or sibling also has the disorder.

Neuroimaging studies have indicated variations in the size of particular brain regions and the amount of activity in areas linked with attention and self-regulation.

Moreover, ADHD is not only about the prevalence of particular behaviors; it's about the persistent and pervasive nature of these symptoms and how they hinder everyday functioning. It's crucial to recognize that ADHD appears differently in each individual, making it a customized experience.

ADHD In Adults Vs. Children

The appearance of ADHD might differ greatly between children and adults. In youngsters, ADHD symptoms commonly include hyperactivity, impulsiveness, and trouble remaining focused on activities.

These symptoms may lead to difficulty in school, such as low academic performance, behavioral disorders, and problems in social relationships.

In adults, however, the appearance of ADHD may be more subtle and sometimes misinterpreted. Adult ADHD may appear as persistent disorganization, time management challenges, difficulty in retaining attention, and impulsivity in decision-making.

Adults with ADHD can struggle with sustaining jobs, managing relationships, and staying on top of everyday chores. Furthermore, there is a growing acknowledgment of the disparities in how ADHD shows in boys and girls. Boys are more likely to be diagnosed with ADHD in childhood, frequently owing to more overt hyperactivity and behavioral difficulties.

In contrast, girls and women with ADHD often display more inattentive symptoms, which might be less visible and, thus, underdiagnosed.

It is understanding ADHD to its fullest means pushing beyond preconceptions and beliefs. It requires understanding the scientific foundation of the condition and appreciating the many ways it presents across different age groups and genders.

This chapter seeks to give a foundation for understanding ADHD, setting the scene for examining tactics and insights in managing and living with ADHD in later chapters.

Chapter 2: Daily Life With ADHD - The Unseen Struggles

Living with ADHD is like navigating a labyrinth with continually changing walls. The issues are numerous and frequently unnoticed by the outside world. This chapter dives into the everyday problems experienced by persons with ADHD, concentrating on organizational challenges, emotional control, relationships, and professional life.

Organizational Challenges

One of the most noticeable problems for persons with ADHD is maintaining organization. This issue goes beyond missing keys or missed appointments; it's a widespread challenge that permeates every part of life.

For a person with ADHD, the brain's executive processes, responsible for organizing and prioritizing activities, perform differently. This typically leads to a distinct style of processing information and arranging tasks.

Imagine standing amid a room packed with dozens of TVs, each airing a different channel at the same volume. This is what it might feel like for someone with ADHD trying to determine which task to start with.

Prioritizing activities may be stressful, and keeping an ordered living or working area might seem like a mammoth endeavor. The ripple consequences of these organizational difficulties are considerable. Mismanagement of time and resources may lead to missed deadlines, misplaced things, and an overall feeling of disorder.

This disarray may severely damage self-esteem and add to the cycle of worry and irritation.

Emotional Regulation And Relationships

ADHD isn't simply about focus issues; it significantly impacts emotional control. People with ADHD frequently experience emotions more deeply and may have a difficult time controlling those sensations. This emotional dysregulation might emerge as rapid mood swings, irritation, or a fast temper.

In relationships, these emotional issues may produce misunderstandings and disputes. The impulsive characteristic of ADHD might lead to expressing things without thinking, which can damage loved ones.

Additionally, the irregularity in attention might be perceived as apathy or neglect, further straining relationships.

Moreover, persons with ADHD typically deal with rejection sensitivity dysphoria — a word used to describe the extreme emotional distress experienced when sensing rejection or criticism. This may make negotiating personal and professional relationships extremely tough since the fear of rejection or criticism can be paralyzing.

Navigating Professional Life

The working environment, with its focus on timeliness, organization, and constant performance, may be especially tough for those with ADHD.

The regular 9-to-5 routine may seem confining and might worsen ADHD symptoms. Managing deadlines, multitasking, and protracted meetings are common difficulties.

For many individuals with ADHD, maintaining a regular performance at work is a considerable issue. They may excel in spurts of hyperfocus when they get profoundly immersed in a task to the exclusion of everything else. However, retaining this attention over time, particularly on less appealing work, may be draining and frequently unsustainable.

Workplace adjustments and understanding from employers and coworkers may make a major impact. Simple modifications like flexible work hours, a quiet workstation, or organizational tools may boost productivity and well-being.

Unfortunately, the lack of understanding and stigma surrounding ADHD frequently means that many people suffer in secret without getting the care they need.

The everyday existence of someone with ADHD includes managing a range of difficult problems. From organizational challenges to emotional control and professional impediments, these battles are frequently overlooked and misunderstood.

Recognizing and treating these factors is key to building successful techniques for living with ADHD, which we shall discuss in the coming chapters.

Chapter Three: The ADHD Mind - A Different Perspective

Living with ADHD is generally presented as a continual fight, focused on the obstacles and deficiencies. However, there is another side to this tale — one that illustrates the particular capabilities and creative possibilities of the ADHD mind. This chapter discusses the positive features of ADHD, advocating a change in perspective to discover and exploit these often-overlooked talents.

Recognizing Your Strengths

The first step in respecting the ADHD mind is understanding the inherent qualities that come with it. Individuals with ADHD frequently display incredible resiliency.

Having traversed a world that isn't created for their neurodiverse brain, individuals can adapt and survive. This perseverance is a valuable asset, particularly when channeled toward personal and professional objectives.

Another important talent is the capacity to think beyond the box. The ADHD mind doesn't follow standard thinking patterns, which may lead to inventive problem-solving and unusual ideas.

This creative thinking may greatly benefit sectors that appreciate innovation and unique ideas. Hyperfocus, a typical feature in persons with ADHD, allows for extreme attention on things of high interest.

While typically perceived as a double-edged sword, this skill may lead to great results in particular areas, especially when paired with personal interests or abilities.

Creativity And ADHD

Creativity is frequently a natural partner of the ADHD mind. It arises from the capacity to find uncommon connections, perceive patterns others may overlook, and think in a non-linear approach.

Many artists, singers, entrepreneurs, and innovators with ADHD have ascribed their creative accomplishments to the unusual way their brain processes.

This creative skill is not confined to the arts; it emerges in daily problem-solving, comedy, and the capacity to tackle life difficulties from novel perspectives. Encouraging and cultivating this creativity may lead to pleasant experiences and unique achievements in numerous disciplines.

Reframing ADHD Traits Positively

An important component of exploiting the positives of ADHD is the positive reframing of qualities generally perceived negatively. For example, impulsivity might be reframed as spontaneity and the capacity to take chances.

While it's crucial to regulate impulsivity to prevent bad outcomes, it may also be a source of vigor and bravery to attempt new things.

Similarly, the propensity to grow rapidly bored with monotonous jobs may be regarded as a desire for novelty and invention. It motivates people to seek out experiences and continually learn, resulting in a wide and diversified collection of skills and knowledge.

Inattention, another feature of ADHD, might be reframed as a sort of mental flexibility. It provides for a greater field of observation and the capacity to change focus swiftly, which may be useful in dynamic circumstances where adaptation is crucial.

In conclusion, the ADHD mind, when understood and accepted, provides a rich tapestry of talents and creative potential. This chapter tries to transform the narrative from one of deficiency to one of variety and competence.

Recognizing, accepting, and using these qualities may lead to a more satisfying and successful life for persons with ADHD.

Chapter Four: Strategies For Success - Practical Tips And Tools

Living with ADHD involves unique obstacles, but it also opens the door to creative tactics and solutions that may dramatically enrich everyday living.

This chapter is devoted to practical, tangible tactics and lifestyle adjustments to fit the ADHD mind.

From time management to attention and distraction management, along with critical lifestyle modifications, we examine strategies to convert ADHD obstacles into opportunities for success.

Time Management Techniques

Effective time management is sometimes a huge challenge for those with ADHD. Traditional tactics may not mesh well with the ADHD brain, asking for more personalized ways.

1. *Visual Time Management:* The ADHD mind reacts strongly to visual signals. Visual time management tools like color-coded calendars, optical clocks, and charts may make abstract notions like time more tangible and approachable.

2. *Breaking Projects Down:* Large projects may be daunting. Breaking things into tiny, manageable portions might make them less frightening.

Using a step-by-step method not only makes jobs more attainable but also gives a clear path and a feeling of success with each minor win.

3. *Time Buffering:* It's typical for persons with ADHD to underestimate the time required for activities. Building in additional time as a buffer may minimize stress and enhance timeliness.

4. *Prioritization Techniques:* Utilizing techniques like the Eisenhower Box may aid in classifying jobs based on urgency and priority, ensuring that vital chores are not ignored.

Focus And Distraction Management

Maintaining attention and avoiding distractions are fundamental issues for persons with ADHD. The following tactics may be extremely effective:

1. *Controlled Atmosphere:* Creating a work atmosphere favorable to concentration is vital. This might mean a clutter-free environment, noise-canceling headphones, or a place away from high-traffic areas.

2. *Technology To Assist Focus:* Various programs are meant to improve focus, such as Pomodoro clocks or apps that block distracting websites during work hours.

3. *Customized Breaks:* Regular, planned breaks may be incredibly useful. These pauses should be scheduled and intentional, enabling the mind to relax without drifting too far off course.

4. *Mindfulness Practices:* Techniques like mindfulness and meditation may boost concentration over time by teaching the brain to redirect attention and reject distractions.

Lifestyle Changes And Habits

Lifestyle modifications may play a key role in treating ADHD symptoms. Consistent routines and good behaviors may give the structure and balance required.

1. _Regular Exercise:_ Physical exercise is excellent for the ADHD brain. It may boost focus, lessen anxiety and depression symptoms, and promote general brain health.

2. _Balanced Diet:_ A diet rich in protein, complex carbs, and omega-3 fatty acids may favorably influence brain function and ADHD symptoms.

3. _Sleep Hygiene:_ Quality sleep is crucial. Establishing a regular sleep pattern and establishing a comfortable resting environment may dramatically improve ADHD treatment.

4. _Stress Management:_ Chronic stress may increase ADHD symptoms. Incorporating stress-reduction practices like yoga, deep breathing exercises, or indulging in hobbies may be immensely useful.

5. *Building Routines:* Establishing and following daily routines may give structure and predictability, decreasing the cognitive burden of decision-making.

6. *Accountability Systems:* Creating accountability mechanisms, whether via apps, diaries, or support groups, may give the required incentive and reminder to keep to routines and objectives.

7. *Conscious Drinking And Caffeine Intake:* Being aware of the use of alcohol and caffeine is vital since they may alter sleep patterns and anxiety levels.

8. *Organizational Tools:* Utilizing calendars, apps, or digital reminders may be a game-changer.

These tools aid in keeping track of appointments, tasks, and deadlines, eliminating the mental stress of needing to recall every detail.

9. *Habit Stacking:* Incorporating new habits by stacking them upon old ones might make them simpler to acquire. For instance, practicing a few minutes of meditation soon after brushing your teeth in the morning may develop a smooth pattern.

10. *Decluttering And Organizing:* A messy environment may be a source of tension and distraction. Regularly arranging and tidying your living and working environments may provide a more soothing and focused atmosphere.

11. *Social Support:* Building a supportive social network, whether it's friends, family, or ADHD support groups, may give encouragement and understanding.

Sharing experiences and techniques with those who understand may be immensely affirming and useful.

12. *Professional Help:* Consulting with ADHD coaches, therapists, or counselors specializing in ADHD may give specific methods and support.

13. *Setting Realistic Objectives:* Setting reasonable, realistic objectives may reduce emotions of overload and failure. Celebrating modest victories may build confidence and drive.

14. *Self-Compassion:* It's necessary to exercise self-compassion. Understanding that some days will be better than others and being fair to oneself during hard times is key.

15. *Cognitive Behavioral Strategies:* These strategies may aid in confronting negative thinking patterns and behaviors linked with ADHD, developing a more positive mentality and approach to obstacles.

16. *Limit Multitasking:* While the ADHD mind could be driven to multitasking, it frequently leads to diminished productivity and greater stress. Focusing on one activity at a time may be more successful.

17. Regular Health Check-Ups: Regular check-ups with healthcare experts help ensure that any connected health concerns are addressed and ADHD medication (if needed) is successfully controlled.

18. Mindfulness In Daily Activities: Incorporating mindfulness into daily activities may increase attention and decrease impulsivity. This may entail entirely focused on a meal, a discussion, or a stroll without interruptions.

19. Creative Outlets: Engaging in creative pursuits may be a therapeutic method to harness the distinctive energy and cognitive processes of ADHD.

20. Learning And Development Mentality: Embracing a mentality centered on learning and development may aid in modifying techniques over time and determining what works best for the person.

Addressing ADHD is not about one-size-fits-all solutions. It's about experimenting with numerous methods, tools, and lifestyle adjustments to discover what matches your thinking best. Remember, the objective is not to erase ADHD qualities but to harness them to promote your life and well-being.

Chapter Five: Building A Supportive Environment

Navigating life with ADHD may be a lonesome road, but it doesn't have to be. Building a supportive atmosphere is crucial to controlling ADHD successfully. This chapter covers developing a caring environment via effective communication with family and friends, getting professional treatment, and creating a solid ADHD support network.

Communicating With Family And Friends

Open and honest communication with family and friends is vital for developing a supportive atmosphere.

For individuals with ADHD, the myths and misunderstandings around the disorder may contribute to feelings of isolation or being misunderstood. Here's how to cross that gap:

1. *Educate Your Loved Ones:* Share information on ADHD with your family and friends. These might be articles, books, or movies that correctly reflect life with ADHD. Education creates understanding and empathy.

2. *Express Your Needs Clearly:* Be explicit about what sort of help you need. Whether it's patience when you're struggling to concentrate, understanding when you're overwhelmed, or aiding with organizing duties, stating your requirements may empower your loved ones to assist you efficiently.

3. Create limits: It's crucial to create healthy limits. Let your loved ones know what is beneficial and what isn't, and don't be ashamed to ask for space when needed.

4. Regular Check-Ins: Establish a system for regular check-ins with close ones. These may be occasions to address what's working, what's not, and any modifications that need to be done.

5. Couples Or Family Therapy: For people in couples or families, therapy may be a good venue to develop communication methods and comprehend one another's views.

Seeking Professional Help

Professional assistance is typically a cornerstone of properly controlling ADHD. Here are some methods to seek out the correct type of expert support:

1. *Find The Right Specialist:* Look for a therapist, psychologist, or psychiatrist specializing in ADHD. They are more likely to recognize the subtleties of the problem and give suitable solutions.

2. *ADHD Coaching:* Consider an ADHD coach. They may give specific techniques to enhance organizational time management and help you remain on track with your objectives.

3. *Group Therapy:* Participate in group therapy sessions. These meetings may give a feeling of camaraderie, as well as insight into how others manage their ADHD.

4. *Medication Treatment:* If medication is part of your treatment strategy, frequent appointments with a psychiatrist or medical practitioner are vital to assess its efficacy and make any required modifications.

5. *Occupational Therapy:* Occupational therapists may aid in establishing ways to handle everyday chores and enhance functioning at home and on the job.

Building Your ADHD Support Network

Beyond family, friends, and professionals, developing a larger ADHD support network may give extra levels of support and understanding.

1. *Join ADHD Support Groups:* Look for local or online support groups. These communities give a forum to exchange experiences, insights, and support with people who understand what you're going through.

2. *Online Forums And Social Media:* Engage with ADHD communities on platforms like Reddit, Facebook, or Twitter. These may be important resources for guidance, information, and a feeling of belonging.

3. ADHD Workshops And Seminars: Attend workshops and seminars on ADHD. They may be good for learning new coping skills and keeping updated about the latest research and therapies.

4. Peer Mentoring: Connect with someone who has been treating ADHD effectively for a longer period. A mentor may give practical guidance, share their experiences, and provide inspiration from a position of empathy.

5. Volunteering In ADHD Communities: Volunteering with groups that concentrate on ADHD awareness and support may be a meaningful way to contribute to the community while also growing your personal support network.

6. *Advocacy Organizations:* Joining or supporting ADHD advocacy organizations may aid in pressing for improved awareness, resources, and legislation to enhance the lives of persons with ADHD.

7. *Networking Events For ADHD Professionals:* Attend events where you may meet professionals who deal with ADHD clients. This might include therapists, coaches, educators, and researchers. Networking with these experts may bring useful insights and resources.

8. *Educational Institutions:* If you are in school or college, use resources like student disability services, which may give help unique to educational settings.

9. *Workplace Support Networks:* If feasible, interact with or build a support network. This may aid in creating an understanding atmosphere and can be a source of support during hard times.

10. *Collaborative Projects With ADHD Peers:* Collaborate on projects with individuals who have ADHD. Such interactions may lead to new methods and a common knowledge of work styles and difficulties.

11. *ADHD-Friendly Social Activities:* Participate in social activities that are ADHD-friendly. Activities that are participatory, engaging, and allow for mobility might be more pleasurable and less stressful.

12. ***Blogs And Podcasts:*** Follow blogs, podcasts, and YouTube channels devoted to ADHD. These may give information, anecdotes, and recommendations about your experiences.

13. ***Regular Meets:*** Organize or participate in regular meets with individuals who have ADHD. These meetings may be casual events where you share stories, provide support, and enjoy the company of those who understand.

14. ***Shared Learning Settings:*** Engage in learning settings or programs that concentrate on skills good for ADHD management, such as organizational skills, mindfulness, or art therapy.

15. *Family Involvement In Community Events:* Involve your family in community events relating to ADHD. This not only helps them comprehend your world better but also enhances your support system.

In building a supportive workplace, it's crucial to realize that every individual's requirements and preferences are distinct. What works for one individual may not work for another.

The idea is to explore numerous help paths and discover the mix that best matches your particular experience with ADHD.

By developing a strong support network, you set the path for a more understanding, accommodating, and empowering environment that not only helps you manage ADHD but also flourishes with it.

Chapter Six: Overcoming Internalized Ableism And Stigma

Navigating life with ADHD sometimes means facing not only the symptoms of the disease but also the internalized ableism and cultural stigma associated with it. This chapter looks into understanding and battling self-stigma, empowering oneself, and the role of activism and awareness in transforming beliefs regarding ADHD.

Understanding And Combating Self-Stigma

Self-stigma arises when persons with ADHD absorb the negative stereotypes and misunderstandings common in society regarding their disease.

This may lead to humiliation, inadequacy, and a skewed self-image.

1. Recognize The Indications Of Self-Stigma: The first step in battling self-stigma is recognizing its indications. This may involve negative self-talk, downplaying one's talents, or feeling humiliated for requiring accommodations or aid.

2. Educate Yourself About ADHD: Knowledge is a great weapon against stigma. Understanding the scientific realities regarding ADHD might help remove misunderstandings you may have acquired.

This includes identifying ADHD as a valid neurodevelopmental condition with particular brain function and structural features.

3. Confront Negative Ideas: Actively engage negative ideas and attitudes about yourself. When a bad notion occurs, consider it critically. Replace it with a more realistic and positive attitude.

4. Celebrate Tiny Wins: Recognize and celebrate your victories, no matter how tiny. This aids in creating confidence and a good self-image.

5. Seek Supportive Therapy: Cognitive-behavioral therapy (CBT) and other therapeutic techniques may aid in confronting and reframing negative thoughts about oneself.

Empowering Yourself

Empowerment is crucial to conquering the hurdles given by ADHD and cultural stigma. It means embracing your identity with ADHD, harnessing your skills, and advocating for your needs.

1. *Build On Your Strengths:* Focus on your strengths and interests. Every person with ADHD has distinct strengths and abilities. Identify and discover methods to integrate them into your everyday life and work.

2. *Develop Self-Advocacy Skills:* Learn to advocate for oneself in many circumstances, such as in the workplace, school, or social situations. This involves discussing your requirements and the adjustments that might benefit you.

3. *Create A Tailored Management Strategy:* Develop a tailored strategy for controlling your ADHD. This should contain solutions that work for you, whether organizational tools, lifestyle modifications, or coping processes.

4. *Practice Self-Care:* Prioritize self-care. This involves providing appropriate sleep, nourishment, exercise, and time for relaxation. Self-care is vital for preserving mental and physical wellness.

5. *Create limits:* Learn to develop healthy limits. Say no to things that overwhelm you or detract from your well-being.

Advocacy And Awareness

Advocacy and spreading awareness are crucial in eliminating the stigma surrounding ADHD. They entail educating people, challenging misconceptions, and fostering a more inclusive and understanding society.

1. *Share Your Story:* If you're comfortable, share your experiences with ADHD. Personal tales are significant instruments in shifting perspectives and developing understanding.

2. *Educate People:* Take chances to educate people about ADHD. This might be via casual discussions, social media, blogging, or involvement in community activities.

3. *Support ADHD Advocacy Groups:*

Support or join ADHD advocacy organizations and campaigns. These organizations strive for increased knowledge, better legislation, and more assistance for those with ADHD. Being part of such movements may be uplifting and help bring about social change.

4. *Confront Misunderstandings:*

Whenever you hear myths or misunderstandings regarding ADHD, whether in personal interactions or public venues, confront them with facts and personal observations. This assists in progressively influencing public perception.

5. *Participate In Awareness Campaigns:*

Participate in or organize awareness campaigns, workshops, or seminars regarding ADHD.

These may be platforms to educate the public, provide information, and interact with others.

6. Collaborate With Educators And Companies: Work with educators and companies to create more ADHD-friendly settings. This might entail pushing for legislation changes, adjustments, or delivering training sessions on ADHD.

7. Promote Inclusive Language: Encourage using inclusive and polite language when dealing with ADHD. Words impact perception and good words may help lessen stigma.

8. Use Social Media For Awareness: Utilize social media channels to promote awareness about ADHD.

This may be an effective strategy to reach a bigger audience and influence narratives regarding ADHD.

9. *Encourage Research And Scientific Inquiry:* Support or participate in research activities to understand ADHD better. Scientific study may give the facts required to fight falsehoods and prejudices.

10. *Engage In Artistic Expression:* Use art, music, writing, or other forms of creative expression to describe the ADHD experience. Art may be a powerful tool to communicate, educate, and connect with others.

11. *Foster Community Engagement:* Engage in community activities and debates regarding mental health and neurodiversity.

Building a community-focused strategy may aid in establishing a more inclusive society.

12. *Be A Role Model:* By managing your ADHD properly and having a meaningful life, you become a role model for others. Showing that it's possible to flourish with ADHD might inspire and motivate others.

13. *Mentorship:* If feasible, mentor individuals battling with ADHD. Sharing your experiences, solutions, and understanding might be useful to someone experiencing similar issues.

14. *Advocate For Accessible Resources:* Advocate for more accessible resources for persons with ADHD, whether in healthcare, education, or the job.

15. Normalize Talks About Mental Health: Help in normalizing discussions about mental health and neurodiversity in your groups. Open talks may lead to increased understanding and acceptance.

By combining self-empowerment with advocacy and awareness initiatives, we may not only better our lives but also pave the path for a more tolerant and understanding society.

Overcoming internalized ableism and stigma is not simply a personal journey; it's a social endeavor that demands tenacity, grit, and a lot of heart.

Chapter Seven: The Power Of Community And Shared Experiences

In the journey of living with ADHD, one of the most important sources of strength and understanding comes from the community. This chapter addresses the transforming impact of connecting with people with similar experiences, learning from their tales, and lending your voice to the collective story.

Finding And Engaging With The ADHD Community

Discovering a community that understands the subtleties of living with ADHD may be life-changing. Here's how you may locate and interact with such communities:

1. Online Forums And Social Media: The internet contains various tools and communities for those with ADHD. Platforms like Reddit, Facebook, and Twitter feature various ADHD communities where members exchange advice, experiences, and support.

2. Local Support Groups: Many cities and towns provide support groups for persons with ADHD. These groups frequently meet regularly and may offer a venue for discussing experiences and tactics face-to-face.

3. Conferences And Workshops: Attending ADHD conferences and workshops is a terrific way to meet people in the community. These events generally include speakers who are experts in the subject and allow the acquisition of new knowledge and ideas.

4. ADHD Coaching And Therapeutic Groups: Participating in groups run by ADHD coaches or therapists may give organized support and a feeling of community.

5. School And University Groups: If you're a student, there are ADHD support groups on campus. These may be useful tools for handling the special issues of ADHD in academic contexts.

6. Volunteering With ADHD Organizations: Volunteering with organizations focusing on ADHD may help you connect with enthusiastic people about the same subject.

Learning From Others' Stories

There's great power in shared tales. They not only give comfort but also provide insights and learning opportunities.

1. Listening To Personal Experiences: Hearing about others' experiences with ADHD may create a feeling of connection and understanding. It reminds you that you're not alone in your troubles and triumphs.

2. Gaining Varied angles: The ADHD community is mixed, and connecting with it may help you view the disease from other angles. This may be especially informative regarding learning how ADHD affects individuals of various ages, genders, and origins.

3. Learning New Techniques: Often, the finest advice and techniques come from people who have experienced the event. Learning what has worked for others might offer you new skills to manage your symptoms.

4. Finding Inspiration And Hope: Stories of overcoming problems and accomplishing objectives may be tremendously encouraging. They may bring hope and inspiration on tough days.

Contributing Your Voice

While learning from others is vital, there's also enormous value in offering your voice to the community.

1. Sharing Your Story: Sharing your story with ADHD may empower you and your listeners. It assists in developing relationships and might give others ideas or methods they hadn't considered.

2. Offering Support And Encouragement: Just as you benefit from the community's support, your encouragement and understanding might be a lifeline for others.

Offering a kind word, sharing your coping strategies, or simply being there to listen may tremendously impact someone's life.

3. Blogging Or Vlogging: Consider beginning a blog or vlog about your ADHD experiences.

This not only helps in processing your ideas and emotions but also extends out to a larger audience, providing them with someone they can connect to.

4. *Participating In Conversations:* Active engagement in community conversations, whether online or in person, adds to the depth of the community. Your unique viewpoint and experiences may bring significant insights to these talks.

5. *Becoming A Community Advocate:* If you're comfortable, take on a more active role by becoming an advocate within the ADHD community.

This might entail organizing events, directing support groups, or pushing for ADHD awareness and accommodation in schools and workplaces.

6. *Mentoring:* If you've navigated ADHD for some time, try mentoring someone recently diagnosed. Your counsel may help them traverse the early stages of recognizing and managing ADHD.

7. *Giving Workshops Or Seminars:* If you have skills or experiences that might help others, try giving workshops or seminars. This may be a forum to exchange tactics and insights and share knowledge regarding ADHD.

8. *Collaborative Initiatives:* Engage in initiatives that enhance the ADHD community. This might be research, awareness campaigns, or generating materials like books or manuals.

9. *comments And Advocacy:* Provide remarks or recommendations to organizations and platforms that cater to the ADHD community. Your opinion may help develop more effective resources and policies.

10. *Creative Expression:* Use your creative abilities to express and share your ADHD experience. Art, music, poetry, and other forms of expression may be great instruments for communication and connection.

11. *Networking With Experts:* Connect with ADHD experts, such as therapists and researchers, to share your views.

Your experiences may influence their work and help them better understand and assist the ADHD community.

12. *Hosting Supportive Events:* Organize or organize events, either digitally or in person, for persons with ADHD. These events may be casual and provide a secure area for sharing and fellowship.

13. *Writing Articles Or Opinion Pieces:* Write articles or opinion pieces for blogs, journals, or newspapers on life with ADHD. This promotes awareness and gives a forum for your voice and experiences.

14. *Social Media Advocacy:* Use social media channels to campaign for ADHD awareness and acceptance.

Share your stories, clarify misconceptions, and emphasize the reality of life with ADHD.

15. Participating In Research: Participate in ADHD research studies or surveys. Your participation gives essential data that will aid in understanding ADHD better and creating effective therapies.

By connecting with the ADHD community, learning from shared experiences, and offering your voice, you not only enhance your journey but also play a critical role in developing a supportive, knowledgeable, and empathetic community.

Remember, every tale, including yours, contributes a unique threat to the rich tapestry of the ADHD storyline.

Chapter Eight: From Coping To Thriving — Long-term Growth With ADHD

Living with ADHD is not only about managing the problems; it's about flourishing and attaining long-term progress. This chapter is devoted to converting the ADHD path from one of just surviving to one of thriving and success. We'll cover establishing realistic objectives, accepting change and development, and the value of recognizing minor triumphs.

Setting Realistic Goals

Goal planning is a great tool for anybody, but it is especially crucial for persons with ADHD. Here's how to create reasonable and attainable goals:

1. Understand Your Strengths And Difficulties: Identify your unique strengths and difficulties. This insight can help you develop objectives that are not only hard but also attainable.

2. Set Specific And Measurable Objectives: Vague objectives are hard to attain and more difficult to quantify. Be explicit about what you intend to achieve and create measurable targets.

3. Break Down Large Objectives: Large objectives might be daunting. Break them down into smaller, more doable tasks. This makes it simpler to concentrate and minimizes anxiety.

4. Use Visual Tools: Visual representations of your objectives may be highly powerful. Consider utilizing vision boards, goal charts, or applications that enable you to monitor your progress graphically.

5. Adjust Expectations: Be flexible with your expectations. Understand that certain objectives could take longer than others, and that's alright.

6. Regular Reviews: Periodically evaluate your objectives. This will help you remain on track and make any required modifications.

Embracing Change And Growth

Change is a constant in life, and accepting it may be especially tough for persons with ADHD.

However, recognizing change as a chance for progress may lead to substantial personal improvement.

1. Adopt A Progress Mentality: Embrace a mentality that sees setbacks as opportunities for progress rather than impediments. This mindset supports resilience and tenacity.

2. Gain New talents: Continuously attempt to gain or upgrade old ones. This may be in areas directly connected to controlling ADHD or in any other area of personal or professional interest.

3. Seek Comments: Constructive comments may be useful. Seek input from reputable persons about how you may develop and grow.

4. *welcome New Experiences:* Step out of your comfort zone and embrace new experiences. This may lead to personal development and a wider viewpoint.

5. *Self-Reflection:* Regular self-reflection may help you comprehend your development areas and appreciate how far you've come.

Celebrating Small Wins

Celebrating tiny triumphs is vital in the process of living with ADHD. It assists in creating confidence and retaining motivation.

1. *Acknowledge Your Efforts:* Every effort, no matter how modest, is worth appreciating. Celebrate the fact that you are trying and making progress.

2. *Set Mini-Goals:* Set mini-goals to your bigger objectives. Celebrating these modest victories may create a feeling of accomplishment and raise your attitude.

3. *Share Your Success:* Share your triumphs with friends, family, or support groups. Sharing your triumphs might heighten your feeling of accomplishment.

4. *Reward Yourself:* Give yourself modest prizes for reaching your objectives. This might be anything from a favorite dessert to a peaceful evening. These prizes might act as positive reinforcement, motivating you to continue.

5. *Maintain A Success Diary:* Keep a diary or account of your triumphs and milestones. This may be a wonderful tool to reflect on your progress and keep you encouraged.

6. *Reflect On Your Journey:* Regularly reflect on where you began and how far you've gone. This may create a greater feeling of success and perspective.

7. *Positive Affirmations:* Use positive affirmations to support your accomplishments. Affirmations may assist in altering your thinking from concentrating on obstacles to recognizing and praising your triumphs.

8. *Involve Your Support Network:* Your support network may play a significant part in celebrating your successes. Their appreciation and support may considerably increase your feeling of success.

9. *Visualize Your Progress:* Create a visual representation of your progress, such as a progress bar or a sequence of checkboxes.

Seeing your progress graphically may be very pleasant and inspiring.

10. Celebrate Progress, Not Perfection:
Focus on rewarding progress rather than waiting for perfection. Recognize that every step forward is a success in itself.

11. Develop A Celebration Routine:
Develop a personal routine to celebrate your triumphs, no matter how minor. This might be as simple as a moment of thankfulness or a specific activity you like.

12. Create A Wall Of Successes: Consider devoting a spot in your house or business where you exhibit your accomplishments. This 'wall of achievements' might be a continual reminder of your victories.

13. *Share Your Experience:* Sharing your experience of overcoming problems and attaining objectives may be a celebration. It may also inspire and support others in their endeavor.

14. *Acknowledge Your Development:* Celebrate not only the successes but also the personal development that has come with them. Acknowledge the talents, resilience, and knowledge you've earned.

15. *Appreciate The Moment:* Allow yourself to enjoy and cherish the moment of success thoroughly. Sometimes, just taking the time to revel in the victory may be a tremendous celebration.

Shifting From coping to flourishing with ADHD entails establishing realistic objectives, accepting change and progress, and enjoying every triumph.

These techniques aid in establishing a positive mindset, improving self-esteem, and generating a feeling of empowerment. Remember, each small step is a part of a broader journey towards flourishing with ADHD.

Conclusion: ADHD And The Journey Ahead

As we approach the completion of our study into the realm of ADHD, it's vital to stop and reflect on the adventure we've gone on together. This last chapter tries to integrate the insights and lessons acquired, look ahead to the expanding landscape of ADHD knowledge and understanding, and provide closing words of support for your continued path.

Reflecting On Personal Growth

1. Acknowledging Your Progress: Reflect on how far you've gone since your diagnosis or the beginning of your ADHD adventure. Acknowledge the struggles you've encountered, the barriers you've conquered, and the knowledge you've earned.

2. Personal Development: Consider the personal development you've achieved via controlling your ADHD. This can include better self-awareness, stronger coping methods, and a deeper knowledge of your strengths and flaws.

3. Resilience And Adaptability: Recognize the resilience and adaptability you've acquired. Living with ADHD typically needs ongoing adjustment and learning, abilities that are beneficial in many aspects of life.

4. Relationships And Communication: Reflect on how your experience with ADHD has influenced your relationships. Think about how your communication may have improved and how you've learned to advocate for yourself.

5. *Self-Acceptance:* Consider how your attitude towards yourself and your ADHD has changed. Celebrate the amount of self-acceptance you've attained and how this has positively influenced your life.

Future Prospects For ADHD Awareness And Understanding

1. *Growing Awareness:* The knowledge and awareness of ADHD continue to rise. I look forward to a future when ADHD is more generally acknowledged and better understood by the general population.

2. *Advancements in Research:* Stay hopeful about present and future research on ADHD.

These investigations hope to provide deeper insights into the illness, leading to more effective management tactics and therapies.

3. *Improved Support Systems:* Anticipate advances in support systems, both in educational settings and the workplace. These modifications are likely to produce circumstances where persons with ADHD may flourish more readily.

4. *Increased Advocacy:* The development of advocacy movements and awareness campaigns promises a future where the needs and rights of persons with ADHD are more actively championed and preserved.

5. *Holistic Ways To Treatment:* Expect a further movement towards more holistic and tailored ways of treating and managing ADHD, emphasizing the individual's unique experiences and needs.

6. *Technology And Innovation:* With the fast expansion of technology, I look forward to novel tools and applications meant to aid in managing many elements of ADHD, from organization to mental health.

7. *Community And Connection:* The burgeoning ADHD community, both online and offline, promises a future of increasing support, shared knowledge, and a feeling of belonging.

Final Words Of Encouragement

1. *Embrace Your Journey:* Your ADHD journey is uniquely yours. Embrace it with all its ups and downs, realizing that each stride, whether forward or backward, is a part of your progress.

2. *You Are Not Alone:* Remember that you are part of a huge and varied group. Many out there understand your hardships and successes. Don't hesitate to reach out and connect.

3. *Celebrate Your Uniqueness:* Your ADHD is a part of what makes you distinct. Celebrate the perspective and creativity it provides to your life.

4. Keep Learning And Growing: Continue to educate yourself on ADHD. The more you understand your brain and its workings, the more you can manage your symptoms and utilize your abilities.

5. Advocate For Yourself And Others: Be an advocate for yourself and others with ADHD. Use your experiences and voice to develop better understanding and empathy, both in your circles and in the larger community.

6. Focus On What Matters: Remember what matters to you. Align your objectives and activities with your beliefs, interests, and what gives you pleasure.

7. Resilience Is Key: Remember, resilience is not about never falling but about getting back up every time you do. Your perseverance is a testimonial to your strength.

8. Seek And Provide Assistance: Don't hesitate to seek help when needed, and equally, be there to support others. Shared experiences and mutual support are important.

9. Maintain A Balanced Perspective: While it's vital to appreciate the problems of ADHD, also recognize the wonderful features and qualities it brings into your life.

10. Embrace Change: Be open to change and progress. Your path with ADHD could develop over time, and being adaptive will help you negotiate these changes successfully.

11. Your Contribution Matters: Never underestimate the significance of your stories and experiences. Sharing your journey may inspire and motivate others.

12. Continual Progress: Remember that progress doesn't always seem linear. There will be good and tough days, but each day is a step towards a deeper knowledge of yourself.

13. Grasp Onto Hope: Finally, hold onto hope. With every new day comes the prospect of fresh discoveries, progress, and delight.

Your ADHD journey is not only about managing; it's about flourishing, learning, and giving in ways only you can. As we close, please take a minute to thank yourself for the guts and work it takes to negotiate life with ADHD.

The path ahead may have difficulties, but it's also loaded with opportunity and promise. With continual self-awareness, support, and advocacy, there's every reason to look toward the future with hope and confidence.

Appendix

The road with ADHD is one of continual learning and adaptation. To assist on this journey, having access to a range of materials is vital.

This appendix contains a complete list of supplementary resources, including books, websites, channels, professional organizations, and support groups that may be important in understanding and treating ADHD.

Books

1. "Driven To Distraction" By Edward M. Hallowell, M.D., and John J. Ratey, M.D.: A revolutionary book that gives insight into the nature of ADHD and solutions for treating it successfully.

2. "Taking Charge Of ADHD" by Russell A. Barkley, Ph.D.: This book deeply explains ADHD and presents scientifically informed treatment techniques.

3. "The ADHD Effect On Marriage" By Melissa Orlov: A wonderful resource for couples suffering from ADHD's effect on their relationship.

4. "Smart But Scattered" by Peg Dawson and Richard Guare: Focused on building executive abilities in children and people with ADHD.

5. "ADHD: What Every Parent Needs to Know" by the American Academy of Pediatrics: A comprehensive resource for parents parenting children with ADHD.

6. *"The Disorganized Mind"* by Nancy A. Ratey: Tailored for adults with ADHD, this book provides solutions for overcoming frequent disorganization and lack of attention.

Websites And Channels

1. ADDitude Magazine (additudemag.com): A premier source for solutions and assistance for ADHD and associated problems.

2. CHADD (Children and Adults with Attention-Deficit/Hyperactivity Disorder) (chadd.org): A nationwide nonprofit organization offering education, advocacy, and support for those with ADHD.

3. How To ADHD (YouTube Channel): A channel devoted to helping people with ADHD and their families manage the illness via interesting and instructive videos.

4. Understood (understood.org): Offers tools and community assistance for persons with ADHD and other learning and attention challenges.

5. ADHD reWired (adhdrewired.com): Provides podcasts, coaching, and an active community for people with ADHD.

6. TotallyADD.com: A website promoting comedy, hope, and useful information regarding adult ADHD.

Professional Organizations

1. *The Attention Deficit Disorder Association (ADDA):* An organization concentrating on the concerns of adults with ADHD. It offers information, resources, and networking opportunities.

2. *The American Professional Association of ADHD and Related Disorders (APSARD):* A professional association concentrating on research and treatment of ADHD.

3. *European Network Adult ADHD:* Offers information and assistance particularly suited to adults with ADHD throughout Europe.

4. *The National Institute of Mental Health (NIMH):* Provides extensive information about ADHD, including the latest research and treatment choices.

Support Groups

1. ADHD Support Groups (via CHADD): Offers local and online support groups for persons with ADHD and their families.

2. ADHD Coaches Organization (ACO): Provides a database of professional ADHD coaches who give help and solutions for managing ADHD.

3. Meetup Groups For ADHD: Platforms like Meetup.com typically feature local groups for those with ADHD to exchange experiences and support one other in person.

4. ADHD Peer Support Groups (Online Platforms): There are various online forums and groups on social media platforms like Facebook, Reddit, and others where persons with ADHD may get peer support.

5. Parents Of Children With ADHD Support Groups: These groups give support and information particularly suited for parents managing children with ADHD.

6. Adult ADHD Support Groups: Aimed at adults with ADHD, these groups concentrate on the particular issues experienced in maturity, giving solutions for coping and flourishing.

7. Young Adults With ADHD Groups: Targeted for teenagers and young adults, these groups give age-appropriate support and assistance.

8. Women With ADHD Support Groups: These groups address the special difficulties and challenges experienced by women with ADHD.

9. Workplace ADHD Support Networks: Some firms provide internal support groups or networks for workers with ADHD.

10. ADHD Support For Educators: Groups and forums devoted to educators who either have ADHD or deal with students with ADHD.

11. International ADHD Organizations: Many nations have their own ADHD organizations offering regional support and services.

12. *ADHD Advocacy Groups:* Groups focusing on advocacy work for ADHD rights, awareness, and accommodations in diverse contexts.

13. *Mental Health Groups:* Many mental health groups and organizations provide information and support for those with ADHD.

14. *Online Webinars And Workshops:* Regularly planned online events that offer education and community participation opportunities.

15. *Family Support Networks:* Support networks for families impacted by ADHD, including help managing relationships, communication, and family dynamics.

By exploring these resources, persons with ADHD and their loved ones may obtain deeper insights, practical methods, and a feeling of community.

These materials provide a wide range of knowledge, from medical and scientific understanding to personal tales and coping strategies, leading to a more holistic approach to treating ADHD.

Whether you seek education, support, or connection, these sites give useful skills and perspectives to assist in navigating the road with ADHD.